AF431137
FUN
FLAMINGO
FACTS
FOR KIDS
by Naomi Hopkins

Adult flamingos are four to five feet tall, but only weigh between four and eight pounds. That's the kind of astonishing body density (or lack of) needed for flight.

FLAMINGOS WINGSPAN RANGES FROM 3.3 - 5 FEET.

The bright colour of flamingo feathers is caused by the presence of carotenoid pigments found in the algae and crustaceans that make up the diet of a flamingo.

The flamingo is a filter-feeder, holding its curved beak upside down in the water it sucks in the muddy water and pushes the mud and silt out the side while tiny hair-like filters along the beak called lamellae sieve food from the water.

Flamingos hold their breath while feeding.

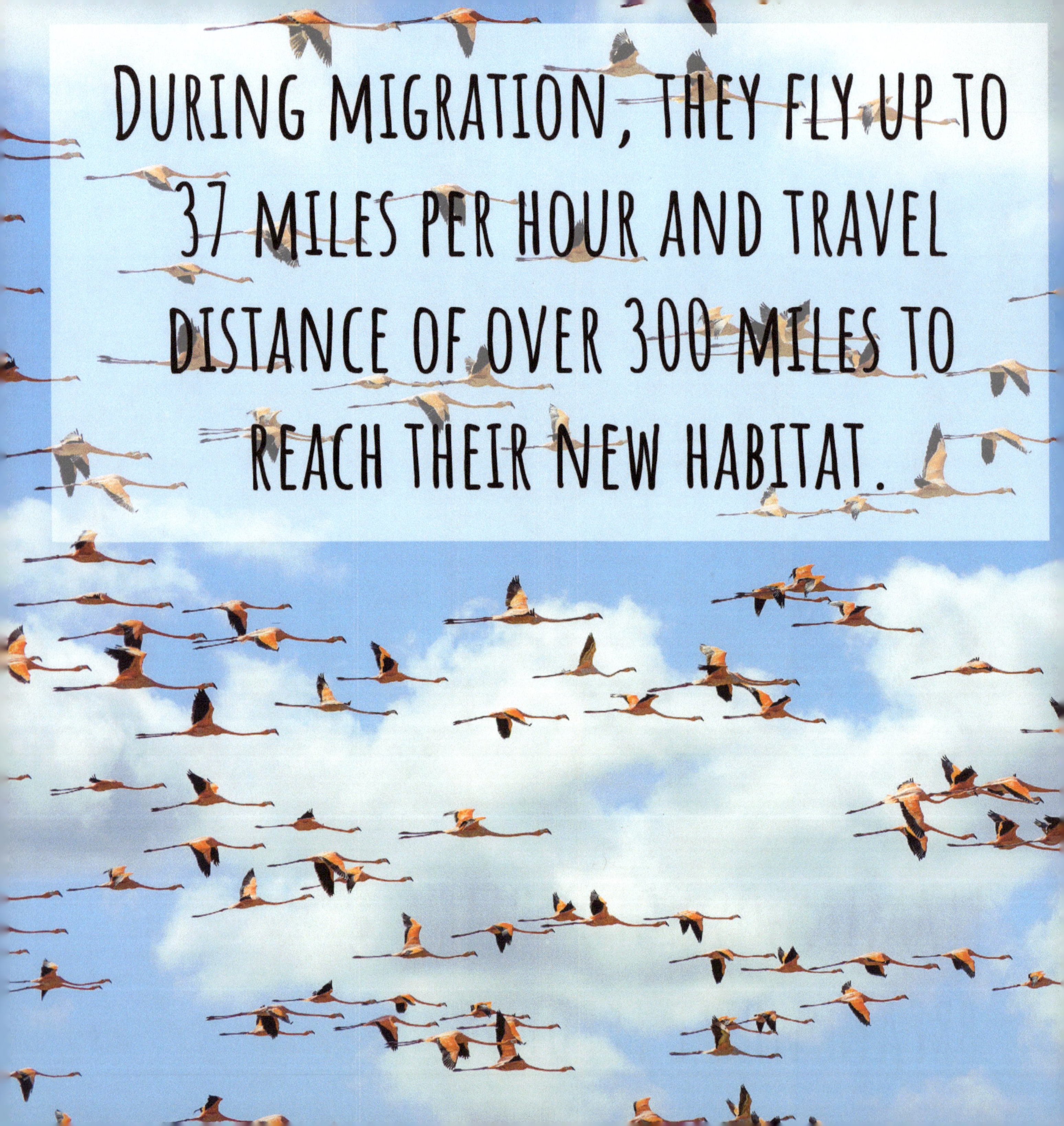
DURING MIGRATION, THEY FLY UP TO
37 MILES PER HOUR AND TRAVEL
DISTANCE OF OVER 300 MILES TO
REACH THEIR NEW HABITAT.

Flamingos spend 15-30% of the day in cleaning their feathers: oil produced in a special gland will be spread over feathers with a help of their beak.

Flamingos live in large groups called colonies. Some colonies consist of million birds.

Flamingos tend to congregate in mudflats or lagoons, where they can find shallow saltwater prey. These habitats are also difficult for predators to negotiate.

The male and female of a mating pair build a nest together, and both sit on the egg while it incubates for about a month.

Little grey baby flamingo chicks hatch atop a mud nest constructed by the adults and take up to three years to attain their full mature plumage. The flamingos become pink over time as their feathers are slowly dyed by the carotenoids in their diet.

When a flamingo chick hatches, both parents take turns feeding it: first with a special liquid baby food they produce in their throats called crop milk, then with regurgitated regular flamingo food as the chick ages.

BABY FLAMINGOS DON'T HAVE CURVED BILL, IT BECOMES CURVED AFTER FEW MONTHS.

Flamingos are monogamous (they have just one partner) and they produce one egg each year.

When they want to rest,
flamingos stand on one leg.

Flamingo legs can be longer than their entire body. The backward bending "knee" of a flamingo's leg is actually its ankle, the knee is out of sight further up the leg.

Flamingos live between 20 and 30 years.

The word 'flamingo' comes from the Spanish word 'flamenco' meaning fire, which refers to the bright pink or orange colour of the feathers.

There are six flamingo species, including the greater flamingo, Chilean flamingo, lesser flamingo, Caribbean flamingo, Andean flamingo and puna flamingo.

The four species in the New World include the Chilean flamingo, found in temperate South American areas, the Andean Flamingo and James's flamingo found in the high Andes mountains in Peru, Chile, Bolivia and Argentina and the American flamingo of the Caribbean islands, Belize and Galapagos islands.

The American flamingo is the only flamingo species native to North America, but is rarely seen in the United States anymore.
It is generally more brightly colored than the Greater flamingo (Phoenicopterus roseus) that inhabits the coasts of Africa, Asia, and southern Europe. Although the Greater flamingo is the most widespread species, the most numerous is the Lesser flamingo.

HE PINKEST BIRDS HAVE THE HIGHEST STATUS IN THE COLONY AS THE BRIGHT COLOUR SHOWS THAT A PARTICULAR INDIVIDUAL IS STRONG AND GOOD AT FINDING FOOD RESOURCES.

DURING A COLONY'S BREEDING TIME, A HIGH RANKING INDIVIDUAL WILL INFLUENCE THE REST OF THE FLOCK TO BREED BY CHANGING ITS FEATHER COLOUR TO A DEEPER PINK, KICK-STARTING THE BREEDING RITUALS.

Flamingos flock in groups of up to several hundred birds. They often perform their mating displays together, like this flamingo flamenco. However, different species and even different flocks will put a slightly different spin on their communal rituals. Read about some of the individual mating dance moves.

The feathers under their wings (flight feathers) are black. You only see them when the birds are flying.

Some flamingos find it easier to steal a nest that's already been built, so mating pairs must guard a nest from other flamingos as well as predators.

A VARIETY OF LAND PREDATORS WILL EAT FLAMINGOS AND THEIR EGGS, BUT SINCE THEIR NESTS ARE BUILT ON SWAMPLAND OR MUDFLATS, THE MOST COMMON PREDATORS FOR FLAMINGOS ARE OTHER BIRDS.

THE FLAMINGO IS THE NATIONAL BIRD OF
THE BAHAMAS.